FINANCIAL FREEDOM IN YOUR 20s AND 30s

A PRACTICAL GUIDE

By

SUNDAY ISAIAH UGBANU

Copyright © [2024] by [SUNDAY ISAIAH UGBANU]
All rights reserved. No part of this publication may be reproduced, distributed, or transmitted in any form or by any means, including photocopying, recording, or other electronic or mechanical methods, without the prior written permission of the copyright holder, except in the case of brief quotations embodied in critical reviews and certain other noncommercial uses permitted by copyright law.

TABLE OF CONTENTS

INTRODUCTION

Why Financial Freedom in Your 20s and 30s Matters

CHAPTER ONE
Setting Your Financial Goals

1.1 Defining Financial Freedom

1.2 how to set realistic, achievable goals

CHAPTER TWO
Smart Budgeting for Beginners

2.1 Basic Budgeting Steps

2.2 Tips for Sticking to Your Budget

CHAPTER THREE
Paying Off Debt Quickly

3.1 Strategies for Paying Off Student Loans, Credit Cards, and Other Debt

3.2 Building Credit for the Future

CHAPTER FOUR
Simple Investing for Young Adults

4.1 Basics of Investing

4.2 How to Start with a Small Amount.

CHAPTER FIVE
Paying Off Debt Quickly

5.1 Side Hustles and Passive Income Ideas.

5.2 Earning More in Your Free Time

CHAPTER SIX
Planning for the Future

6.1 Starting Your Retirement Fund Early

6.2 Financial Independence Basics

CONCLUSION

INTRODUCTION

Why Financial Freedom in Your 20s and 30s Matters

If you're here, you're probably dreaming about a life where money isn't a constant worry. Maybe you want to travel, start a business, or simply live comfortably without feeling chained to a paycheck. Whatever your goals, the idea of financial freedom sounds appealing, right?

But here's the truth: achieving financial freedom, especially in your 20s and 30s, isn't just about having more money. It's about creating options. When you're financially free, you're able to make choices that aren't dictated by stress or financial obligations. You have room to explore opportunities, take on new challenges, and live a life that's truly yours.

Now, you might be thinking, "Isn't financial freedom for older, wealthier people?" Not at all! The sooner you start, the more time you have to build and grow your money. This is why your 20s and 30s are the perfect time to begin. Every small step you take now, every dollar you save, and every smart choice you make will add up over time.

In this guide, "FINANCIAL FREEDOM IN YOUR 20s AND 30s" we're going to explore practical, easy-to-follow steps to get you closer to financial freedom. I'm not talking about fancy financial jargon or complicated formulas. You don't need to be a finance expert to start; all you need is a willingness to learn and a commitment to taking control of your future.

We'll keep things simple, direct, and—hopefully—a bit fun. After all, your financial journey is part of your life's adventure. So let's dive in and start building a financial foundation that will serve you for years to come. However at the end of this guide, you'll have the tools and confidence to make informed financial decisions that can change the course of your life.

CHAPTER ONE

Setting Your Financial Goals

1.1 *Defining Financial Freedom*

Let's start with a question: What does financial freedom actually mean to you? Take a second to think about it. For some people, financial freedom might mean never worrying about rent or bills. For others, it could mean saving enough to travel the world, retire early, or just live comfortably without stress.

In simple terms, financial freedom means having control over your money instead of feeling like it controls you. It's that point where you can comfortably cover your needs, enjoy some wants, and have enough saved or invested to weather life's unexpected twists. It's about choice.

Financial freedom gives you the power to decide where you live, how you spend your time, and what kind of lifestyle you want.
But here's a little secret: financial freedom doesn't have to mean being rich. It's more about being intentional

with the money you have and setting up a system that helps your money grow over time. Think of it as building a solid financial safety net, so you have options and security, no matter what life throws at you.

So, if financial freedom looks different for everyone, how do you know what it means for you? A good place to start is by picturing your ideal life. What would a "financially free" version of your life look like? Would you have a cozy home of your own? Be free from debt? Maybe it's working a job you're passionate about, or even not working at all! When you can visualize this, you'll start to see what you're working toward—and that's the key.

Financial freedom is a journey, and like any journey, it's easier to get where you're going when you know your destination. The rest of this guide will show you how to make steady progress toward your version of freedom. Don't worry about perfection or rushing. As long as you're moving forward, you're already ahead. So take a deep breath, and let's start defining what financial freedom means for you.

Financial freedom is about more than just paying bills or saving money. It's really a mindset shift—seeing money as a tool that enables you to create the life you want, rather than something that limits you. Picture this: financial freedom is like being in the driver's seat of your life. Instead of working endless hours to meet immediate needs, you're able to make choices that support your long-term vision.

When you're financially free, you're not stressing about every little expense or paycheck. You have room to make decisions that fulfill your goals and align with your values. You can pursue interests that bring you joy, support causes you believe in, and invest in experiences that add meaning to your life.

One thing to remember, though, is that financial freedom doesn't happen overnight. It's a gradual process, built on small, consistent habits. Each time you save a little, invest wisely, or make a thoughtful decision about your spending, you're laying a brick in the foundation of your future freedom. And this foundation grows stronger over time, becoming a powerful support system that keeps you grounded even when life is uncertain.

To many, financial freedom also means peace of mind. Imagine knowing that if an emergency hits, you have savings to fall back on. Or that if you suddenly wanted to change careers, take a sabbatical, or start a family, you'd have the resources to make it happen comfortably. Financial freedom provides the flexibility to make those life choices confidently, without the fear of financial strain.

A crucial part of this journey is understanding that your path to financial freedom might look different from someone else's. Some people may aim for early retirement, while others might want to work part-time on projects they're passionate about. Your definition of financial freedom is personal and unique, and it's important to embrace that.

So, as you move through this guide, keep a clear vision of what financial freedom looks like for you. Think about how you want to feel about money—not just today, but years down the line. Let that vision become your guide as you set goals, create habits, and take steps toward your financial freedom. With a clear idea of where you want to go, every action you take becomes a meaningful step forward, bringing you closer to the financial independence you envision.

1.2 *how to set realistic, achievable goals*

Now that you've defined what financial freedom looks like for you, let's talk about setting goals that will actually get you there. A lot of people have dreams of wealth or financial independence, but without clear, realistic goals, those dreams can feel out of reach. The good news? Setting financial goals doesn't have to be complicated. In fact, the simpler and more specific you make them, the better!

First, start by breaking down your vision of financial freedom into smaller, manageable pieces. If your ultimate goal is to have, say, a six-month emergency fund, or to be debt-free, think about the smaller steps it'll take to reach that point. Setting short-term goals makes big financial goals feel less overwhelming, and each small win builds your confidence and motivation.

Let's use an example. If your goal is to save $5,000 in an emergency fund, think of how much you could realistically save each month. If $200 per month feels doable, then aim for that. It may not seem like much at first, but after a year, that's $2,400—nearly halfway to your goal! By focusing on what you can realistically achieve each month, you're setting yourself up for success instead of frustration.

Another tip: make your goals as specific as possible. Instead of saying,

"I want to save more," try "I want to save $1,000 in the next six months by setting aside $170 a month." Notice how specific that is? You know exactly what you're aiming for, how long it will take, and what steps you'll need to take each month. This kind of clarity helps you track your progress and stay motivated.

Be sure to balance your goals with flexibility. Life can be unpredictable—an unexpected expense may pop up, or you might need to adjust your timeline. That's perfectly okay. When you're setting financial goals, think of them as a roadmap rather than a rigid plan. If you have to take a detour or adjust your timeline, you're still on the journey, just with a new route.

Lastly, reward yourself along the way! Celebrate your progress, no matter how small it may seem. Setting up an emergency fund, paying off debt, or sticking to a budget are huge accomplishments. Take time to recognize each step you take, because these wins fuel your motivation to keep going.

Setting realistic, achievable goals is all about being patient and steady. Each small step you take now brings you closer to financial freedom and a future where you control your money, not the other way around.

One important aspect to remember is that your goals should be personalized to fit your lifestyle and financial situation. Just because someone else is saving aggressively or investing in certain stocks doesn't mean that's the right path for you. Financial goals work best when they align with your values and priorities, so you're motivated to stick with them even when things get tough.

Think of it this way: your goals are like puzzle pieces that, when combined, create a bigger picture of financial freedom. For example, if you value security, building a solid emergency fund might be one of your top priorities. If you're focused on growing wealth, setting a goal to start investing could be the right move. When you tailor your goals to your unique vision of financial freedom, each step feels meaningful and relevant, not forced or unrealistic.

Another key to setting achievable goals is to make them measurable. Let's say you want to reduce your monthly expenses by $100. This is specific and measurable—you know the exact amount you're aiming to cut. At the end of each month, you can easily check if you've met your goal.

This measurability makes it easier to track your progress, adjust your approach if needed, and feel a sense of accomplishment when you achieve it.

And don't overlook the importance of setting a timeline for your goals. When you give yourself a deadline, you create a sense of urgency that can help you stay focused.

For instance, "I want to pay off my credit card in 12 months" is clear, time-bound, and easier to work toward than "I want to pay off my credit card someday." With a timeline in place, you're more likely to take consistent actions to reach your target within the specified time frame.

Finally, consider revisiting your goals regularly. Financial freedom is a journey, and your life circumstances and priorities might shift along the way. Maybe you've reached a savings milestone and want to focus on investing more, or perhaps a career change has shifted your income and spending needs.
If you are checking in with your goals every few months, you can adjust as needed to stay aligned with your vision.

Setting realistic, achievable goals isn't about perfection; it's about creating a flexible plan that fits your life and helps you progress toward financial freedom. Embrace the journey, celebrate each milestone, and remember that every small step adds up.

Each dollar saved, every debt paid down, and each investment made brings you closer to a future where your financial choices are your own.

CHAPTER TWO

Smart Budgeting for Beginners

2.1 Basic Budgeting Steps

Budgeting might sound like a chore, but trust me—it's one of the most powerful tools you can use to take control of your finances.

The great thing about budgeting is that it doesn't require a lot of fancy formulas or tools; all you need is a simple, step-by-step approach to track where your money goes and ensure that you're spending in a way that supports your financial goals.

So, let's break down the basic budgeting steps you need to get started.

1. Track Your Income.
Before you can set a budget, you need to know how much money is coming in each month. This is the foundation of your budget because it tells you how much you have to work with.

If you have a steady paycheck, this is straightforward—you know exactly how much you'll earn each month. If your income varies (like if you're a freelancer or have multiple side hustles), track your income over a few months to find an average. It's important to be realistic about your income, even if it fluctuates, so you can plan accordingly.

2. List Your Expenses
Once you know how much money is coming in, the next step is to see where it's going. Start by making a list of all your monthly expenses. Break them down into two categories:

Fixed Expenses: These are the same every month, like rent, utilities, car payments, insurance, etc.

Variable Expenses: These can change month to month, such as groceries, entertainment, dining out, or gas.

Don't forget about irregular expenses, like annual subscriptions or quarterly bills. You can divide those amounts by 12 to get a monthly average, so you're not caught off guard when those bills come due.

3. *Categorize and Prioritize*
After listing your expenses, it's time to categorize them. For example, you can group your expenses into categories like housing, transportation, food, entertainment, etc. Then, look at each category and

prioritize what's essential and what's not.

Fixed expenses like rent or mortgage are non-negotiable, but there may be room to cut back on variable expenses like eating out or subscriptions you don't use regularly. The goal here is to identify areas where you might be overspending and where you can make adjustments to free up more money for savings, debt repayment, or investing.

4. Set Spending Limits
Based on your income and the list of your expenses, the next step is to assign specific limits to each spending category. For example, you

might decide that you'll only spend $200 on groceries this month or that your entertainment budget will be capped at $100. These spending limits will act as your financial boundaries, ensuring you don't overspend and helping you stick to your goals.

Be realistic when setting these limits. If $100 for groceries feels too tight for you, start at a higher amount and adjust over time. The goal is to create a budget that's sustainable, not one that feels like a punishment.

5. Track Your Spending
Now that you have your budget set, the key to staying on track is to track

your spending throughout the month. This doesn't mean micromanaging every purchase, but it does mean checking in regularly to ensure you're sticking to your limits.

You can do this manually by keeping a spending journal or using apps like Mint or YNAB (You Need A Budget) that automatically sync with your bank accounts and credit cards. The more you track, the more aware you become of your spending habits, which can help you make smarter choices down the road.

6. *Adjust as Needed*
A budget is a living document. If something isn't working, adjust it. If

you're constantly going over your grocery budget, try meal planning or finding cheaper alternatives. If you're underspending in one category, consider shifting that money toward savings or paying off debt.

It's important to stay flexible. Life happens, and things don't always go as planned, but that doesn't mean you've failed at budgeting. The goal is to keep making progress toward your financial freedom, even if that means fine-tuning your budget along the way.

7. Review Your Budget Regularly
Lastly, make it a habit to review your budget every month. This will help

you see what's working, what's not, and where you need to adjust. Regular check-ins will keep you aligned with your goals and help you stay motivated as you see your financial picture improve.

If you follow these basic budgeting steps, you'll be well on your way to mastering your money and creating a foundation for financial freedom. It's not about perfection—it's about progress. The more consistent you are with budgeting, the easier it becomes, and the more control you'll have over your finances.

2.2 Tips for Sticking to Your Budget

Creating a budget is a great first step, but sticking to it is where the real challenge lies. It's easy to overspend or get distracted by unexpected expenses. However, with a few smart strategies, you can stay on track and make budgeting a habit that brings you closer to your financial goals. Here are some practical tips to help you stick to your budget:

1. Set Realistic Expectations
One of the biggest mistakes people make when budgeting is setting unrealistic goals. If you try to cut back too much in one area or

overestimate your ability to save, it can lead to frustration and burnout. Be honest with yourself about what's achievable, especially in the beginning.

Start small and adjust your budget as needed. If you're not used to saving 20% of your income, try starting with 10% and gradually increasing it over time. The key is to set goals that you can actually stick to, which will make it easier to build consistency.

2. Automate Your Savings
One of the best ways to make sure you save is to automate it. Set up automatic transfers from your checking account to your savings or

investment accounts as soon as you get paid. By doing this, you're paying yourself first, and you don't have to think about it.

Automating your savings takes away the temptation to spend that money, and it ensures that you're consistently putting money toward your financial goals. Whether it's for an emergency fund, retirement, or something else, this step can make a big difference in sticking to your budget.

3. Use Cash for Variable Expenses
If you struggle with overspending on categories like food, entertainment, or shopping, try using cash instead of credit or debit cards. When you use

cash, it's easier to see when you're nearing your limit for the month.

Consider using the envelope system, where you place a set amount of cash for each spending category. Once the cash is gone, that's it for the month. This simple method can be incredibly effective for controlling impulse purchases and ensuring you stick to your budget.

4. *Track Your Spending Regularly*
Tracking your spending is crucial for staying on top of your budget. Use budgeting apps like Mint, YNAB, or PocketGuard to track where your money is going in real-time. These apps categorize your expenses,

making it easier to see if you're overspending in any category.

You don't have to track every penny, but check in on your budget regularly—at least once a week. This will help you catch any potential problems early and make adjustments before things get out of hand.

5. Set a "Fun Fund" for Discretionary Spending.
It's important to be flexible with your budget so you don't feel restricted. Life is about balance, and being too strict with your spending can lead to burnout. Set aside a small portion of your budget for "fun" expenses—

whether it's going out to eat, buying clothes, or enjoying a hobby.

If you have a set amount of discretionary spending, you can still enjoy life without feeling guilty. Plus, when you know you have money set aside for fun, you're less likely to overspend in other areas.

6. Reevaluate Your Budget Regularly
Life changes, and so should your budget. Regularly reevaluating your budget allows you to adjust for changes in your income, expenses, or goals. For example, if you get a raise, allocate a portion of that extra income to savings or debt repayment rather than increasing your spending.

Similarly, if you find that certain categories consistently need adjustment, don't be afraid to tweak them. The goal is to create a budget that works for you, not one that feels restrictive or unrealistic. Check in with your budget at least once a month to ensure it's still aligned with your financial goals.

7. Avoid Temptation with a Cooling-Off Period.
Impulse spending is a common challenge when trying to stick to a budget. To combat this, implement a "cooling-off" period. When you feel the urge to buy something non-

essential, give yourself 24-48 hours before making the purchase.

This short waiting period allows you to evaluate whether the purchase is necessary or just an impulse. Often, you'll find that the urge passes, and you'll feel good about saving that money instead of buying something on a whim.

8. Use Budgeting as a Family or Team Effort
If you share your finances with a partner or family, make budgeting a team effort. Sit down together to discuss your financial goals, expenses, and priorities. Having everyone on the same page can

reduce misunderstandings and create a sense of accountability.

When everyone is involved in budgeting, it's easier to stick to the plan because you're all working toward the same goals. Plus, it fosters better communication and can help avoid spending-related conflicts.

9. *Reward Yourself for Meeting Milestones*

Sticking to a budget can be tough, so it's important to celebrate your successes along the way. Set small milestones, like hitting a savings goal or staying under budget for the month, and reward yourself for achieving them.

The reward doesn't have to be big—perhaps a small treat or a fun outing that's within your budget. This positive reinforcement keeps you motivated and makes budgeting feel less like a chore.

10. Stay Focused on Your Long-Term Goals.
Lastly, remember why you're budgeting in the first place. Whether it's saving for a down payment on a house, getting out of debt, or building an emergency fund, staying focused on your long-term financial goals can help you stay disciplined.

When you have a clear vision of what you want to achieve, sticking to your budget becomes easier. Remind yourself regularly of your goals, and use that motivation to push through those moments when temptation arises.

CHAPTER THREE

Paying Off Debt Quickly

3.1 *Strategies for Paying Off Student Loans, Credit Cards, and Other Debt*

When it comes to paying off debt, it's crucial to have a strategy in place, especially if you're dealing with multiple types of debt like student loans, credit cards, or personal loans. The goal is to pay down your debt as quickly and efficiently as possible while minimizing interest payments and reducing financial stress. Let's explore some effective strategies for tackling these common types of debt.

1. The Debt Snowball Method
The debt snowball method is one of the most popular approaches to paying off debt. This strategy focuses on paying off your smallest debt first, regardless of interest rates. Here's how it works:

List all your debts from smallest to largest, regardless of the interest rate.

Focus on paying off the smallest debt as quickly as possible, while making the minimum payments on your other debts.

Once the smallest debt is paid off, move on to the next smallest debt, using the money you were putting toward the first one to pay it down faster.

<u>Continue this process until all your debts are paid off.</u>
The debt snowball method can be highly motivating because you get quick wins as you pay off each debt. The sense of accomplishment can keep you motivated to tackle larger debts. However, it may not be the most cost-effective method in terms

of interest payments, as it doesn't prioritize high-interest debts.

2. *The Debt Avalanche Method*

The debt avalanche method is similar to the debt snowball, but instead of focusing on the smallest debt first, you prioritize paying off the debt with the highest interest rate. Here's how it works:

List your debts from highest to lowest interest rate.
Focus on paying off the debt with the highest interest rate first, while making the minimum payments on your other debts.

Once the high-interest debt is paid off, move on to the next debt with the highest interest rate, and so on.
The debt avalanche method is more cost-effective because it helps you minimize the amount of interest you pay over time. While you might not get the same emotional boost as with the debt snowball method, you'll save money in the long run by reducing the amount you pay in interest.

3. *Consolidation and Refinancing*
Debt consolidation and refinancing are strategies that can make managing your debt easier and may help lower your interest rates.

Debt Consolidation involves combining multiple debts into one loan or credit account, often with a lower interest rate. This simplifies your payments and can reduce the interest you pay over time.

Refinancing is similar but typically refers to loans like student loans or mortgages. By refinancing, you can get a lower interest rate on a new loan to pay off the old debt. This could lead to lower monthly payments or a shorter loan term, both of which can help you pay off your debt faster.

Consolidation and refinancing are particularly useful for student loans or credit cards with high interest rates.

However, be cautious about the terms of the new loan, as they could affect your repayment timeline or overall costs.

4. *Balance Transfers for Credit Card Debt*

If you have high-interest credit card debt, a balance transfer can be a good way to save on interest and pay off your debt faster. This strategy involves transferring the balance from a high-interest credit card to a new card with a lower interest rate, often 0% for an introductory period.

The below is how it works:
Find a credit card with a 0% APR balance transfer offer.

Transfer your high-interest balances to the new card.

Pay off as much as possible before the introductory period ends (usually 12 to 18 months).

Balance transfers can be an excellent way to reduce the amount of interest you're paying and help you pay off your debt faster. However, make sure you're aware of any transfer fees and the regular interest rate that kicks in once the introductory period ends. It's also important to avoid adding new charges to the card, as this could offset the benefits of the balance transfer.

5. Pay More Than the Minimum Payment

It's easy to make the minimum payment on your debt and think you're doing enough, but minimum payments often only cover interest, meaning you won't make significant progress on paying down the principal. To make a dent in your debt, aim to pay more than the minimum whenever possible.

Consider the below strategy:
Start by paying just a little extra each month— even an extra $50 to $100 can make a big difference.

Apply any windfalls (tax refunds, bonuses, gifts) toward your debt. If you are making larger payments, you reduce the principal balance faster, which means you'll pay less in interest over time and get out of debt sooner.

6. *Create a Debt Repayment Plan*

No matter which strategy you choose, it's essential to have a solid plan in place. Creating a clear debt repayment plan helps you stay organized, prioritize your payments, and track your progress. Here's how to build one:

List all your debts: Write down each debt you owe, including the amount, interest rate, and minimum payment.

Choose a strategy: Decide whether the debt snowball, debt avalanche, or another method works best for your situation.

Set realistic goals: Determine how much you can afford to pay each month, and make a plan to allocate that amount toward your debts.

Track your progress: Keep a record of your payments and how much your balances are decreasing. This will help keep you motivated and show you're making progress.

A structured plan helps you stay focused and prevent you from feeling overwhelmed. It also makes it easier to adjust if your circumstances change.

7. *Avoid Taking on New Debt*
While paying off existing debt, it's essential to avoid accumulating new debt. This means putting a freeze on new credit card purchases and making sure you don't take on any new loans unless absolutely necessary. Here are some tips to help you stay debt-free while you're repaying your current obligations:

Cut unnecessary expenses: Review your budget and see if there are areas where you can reduce spending.

Use cash or debit: Limit the temptation to use credit cards by switching to cash or debit for everyday purchases.

Avoid lifestyle inflation: As you pay off debt and your financial situation improves, resist the urge to upgrade your lifestyle by taking on more debt. Focusing on living within your means and avoiding new debt, you'll keep your finances on track and make it easier to pay off existing debt.

3.2 Building Credit for the Future

Building and maintaining good credit is a crucial part of your financial journey. Having strong credit opens doors to better loan terms, lower interest rates, and financial opportunities that can help you achieve your long-term goals. Whether you're just starting to build credit or looking to improve your current score, here's how you can set yourself up for success and build credit for the future.

1. Start with a Secured Credit Card
If you're new to credit or rebuilding after setbacks, a secured credit card can be a great place to start. Unlike traditional credit cards, secured cards require you to make a deposit that serves as your credit limit. This deposit acts as collateral in case you don't pay your bill. Over time, responsible use of a secured card can help you build or rebuild your credit.

Here's how it works:
You make a deposit (often between $200-$500), and this becomes your spending limit.

Use the card for small purchases and pay off the balance in full every month.

As you make timely payments, the credit card company will report your activity to the credit bureaus, helping to build your credit history.
Be sure to choose a secured card with low fees and a reasonable interest rate. After a period of responsible use, you may be able to transition to an unsecured card with better terms.

2. *Make Payments on Time*

The most significant factor that affects your credit score is your payment history. Late or missed payments can have a lasting negative impact on your credit. Therefore, it's crucial to pay your bills on time—every time.

Follow this guide to stay on top of payments:

Set up payment reminders or automate your payments to ensure they're never missed.

If you're unable to pay in full, make at least the minimum payment to avoid late fees and damage to your credit score.

Prioritize bills that impact your credit, such as credit cards, student loans, and mortgages.

Making timely payments not only helps improve your credit score but also demonstrates to lenders that you are a responsible borrower.

3. *Keep Your Credit Utilization Low.* Your credit utilization rate—the percentage of your available credit that you're using—accounts for a significant portion of your credit score. Keeping your utilization low is one of the easiest ways to improve your credit score. Ideally, you want to keep your credit utilization rate below 30%, which means if your credit card

has a $1,000 limit, you should aim to carry a balance of no more than $300.

To maintain a healthy credit utilization rate:
Pay off your balance early to ensure that your credit utilization stays low. Request a credit limit increase if you're able to manage your current balance responsibly. A higher credit limit gives you more available credit, which lowers your utilization rate as long as you don't increase your spending.
Use multiple cards wisely—if you have more than one card, spreading out your spending can help keep the utilization rate on each card low.

Keeping your credit utilization in check, you demonstrate financial responsibility, which boosts your credit score over time.

4. Diversify Your Credit Mix
Lenders like to see that you can handle different types of credit responsibly. A diverse credit mix, which includes credit cards, loans, and even installment payments, can have a positive impact on your credit score. However, don't open credit accounts just for the sake of diversity—only open new accounts when they make sense for your financial situation.
Here's how you can diversify:

Consider a mix of credit cards—for example, a regular credit card and a store card.

Think about other types of credit—such as auto loans, student loans, or a personal loan, depending on your situation.

Be cautious about applying for too much credit at once—each time you apply for a new credit account, it can cause a temporary dip in your credit score, so make sure you're applying for credit strategically.

Having a diverse mix of credit shows lenders that you can responsibly manage various types of debt, which helps boost your credit profile.

5. *Avoid Closing Old Accounts*

The length of your credit history is another important factor in determining your credit score. The longer your credit history, the more trustworthy you appear to lenders. So, when you're thinking about closing credit card accounts or loans, consider the potential impact on your credit score.

Here's why:
Closing old accounts can shorten your credit history, which may lower your score.
If you're not using a card, consider keeping it open with a low or zero balance. This helps maintain your credit history length and can positively influence your score.

If you're tempted to close a card due to high annual fees or lack of use, look for cards with no annual fees or downgrade to a card that doesn't charge fees.

Keep your old accounts open as long as they're in good standing to help build a long and positive credit history.

6. Check Your Credit Reports Regularly.

It's important to monitor your credit reports to make sure everything is accurate and up to date. Mistakes happen, and errors on your credit report can negatively impact your credit score. You're entitled to a free credit report from each of the three major credit bureaus—Experian, TransUnion, and Equifax—once a year.

Here's what you should do:

Request your free credit report at AnnualCreditReport.com.

Look for any discrepancies, such as accounts that don't belong to you, late payments that were reported incorrectly, or inaccurate credit limits.

If you find any errors, dispute them with the credit bureau to get them corrected.

Staying on top of your credit reports, you can address errors quickly and ensure your credit score accurately reflects your financial behavior.

7. *Be Patient and Consistent*

Building credit takes time, especially if you're starting from scratch or working to repair past mistakes.

Credit scores are a reflection of your financial habits over time, so the most important thing you can do is stay consistent.

Avoid rushing into new credit applications—give yourself time to establish good habits.

Continue to make on-time payments, keep your utilization low, and regularly check your reports for any inaccuracies.

Over time, your credit score will rise as you prove yourself to be a reliable borrower.

Patience is key when building credit. Don't get discouraged if you don't see immediate results—just keep up the good habits, and you'll see progress.

CHAPTER FOUR

Simple Investing for Young Adults

4.1 Basics of Investing

So, you're thinking about investing—awesome! For many people in their 20s and 30s, investing feels like stepping into an unfamiliar world full of intimidating terms and a lot of uncertainty. But the truth is, investing doesn't have to be complicated or overwhelming. In fact, you don't need a degree in finance or a fortune to get started. Let's go over the basics in a simple, straightforward way, so you can feel confident taking those first steps toward building wealth.

Why Invest in the First Place?
At its core, investing is about growing your money over time. Think of it as putting your money to work so it can earn more money. Sure, you could just save, but savings accounts typically offer very low interest rates, which means your money doesn't grow very quickly. Investing, on the other hand, gives you a chance to earn a higher return on your money

by placing it in assets like stocks, bonds, or mutual funds.

When you invest, you're aiming for your money to grow over the years, which can help you achieve big goals like buying a house, starting a business, or simply retiring comfortably.

Different Types of Investments
There are many ways to invest, but here are the main categories you'll want to know about:

1. Stocks – When you buy a stock, you're buying a small piece (or share) of a company. If the company does well, your share's value goes up, and

you make money. If it doesn't do well, you could lose money. Stocks can be a bit risky, but they tend to offer higher returns over the long term.

2. *Bonds* – *Bonds are like IOUs.* When you buy a bond, you're lending money to a company or government, and they agree to pay you back with interest over time. Bonds are generally less risky than stocks, but they also usually offer lower returns.

3. *Mutual Funds* – A mutual fund pools money from many investors to buy a mix of stocks, bonds, or other assets. By investing in a mutual fund, you get instant diversification

because your money is spread across multiple investments, which helps reduce risk.

4. *ETFs (Exchange-Traded Funds)* – ETFs are similar to mutual funds, but they trade on the stock exchange, just like individual stocks. They're popular because they offer diversification and can be a low-cost way to invest in a broad range of assets.

5. *Real Estate* – Investing in real estate means buying property (like a home, apartment, or commercial space) to rent out or sell for profit. Real estate can be a good long-term

investment, but it requires more capital and hands-on management.

Understanding Risk and Return
When it comes to investing, risk and return go hand in hand. Generally, the higher the potential return, the higher the risk you're taking on. Stocks, for example, can grow your money significantly, but they can also lose value quickly during market downturns. On the flip side, bonds are typically more stable but offer lower returns.

One of the keys to successful investing is finding a balance between risk and return that matches your comfort level and your goals. If you're young, you have time to ride out the ups and downs of the market, so you might feel comfortable taking on a bit more risk. However, if the thought of losing money makes you anxious, it's okay to start with more conservative investments and increase your risk tolerance as you gain confidence.

Compound Interest: The Power of Starting Early
Here's one of the most exciting things about investing: compound interest. Think of it as earning interest on your interest. When you invest, your money earns returns, and those returns are reinvested, so they start earning returns too. Over time, this snowball effect can help your money

grow faster than just adding to your savings each month.

The earlier you start, the more you can benefit from compound interest. Even if you're only investing a small amount, starting now can have a huge impact by the time you're ready to retire.

<u>Setting Up an Investment Account</u>
If you're ready to start investing, you'll first need an investment account. For beginners, the most common types are brokerage accounts and retirement accounts (like IRAs or 401(k)s).

Brokerage Accounts: These are general investment accounts that you can open with an online broker or through a financial advisor. With a brokerage account, you can buy and sell stocks, bonds, mutual funds, and ETFs. There are no restrictions on when you can withdraw your money, so it's a flexible option if you're saving for mid- or long-term goals.

Retirement Accounts: These accounts, such as an IRA (Individual Retirement Account) or 401(k), are specifically for retirement savings and come with tax benefits. The trade-off is that you usually can't access your money without penalties until you're around retirement age.

However, the tax benefits can help you save more over time.
Both types of accounts have pros and cons, so think about your goals and decide which is the best fit for you.

Diversification: Don't Put All Your Eggs in One Basket.
One of the simplest ways to manage risk when investing is through diversification. This means spreading your investments across different types of assets (like stocks, bonds, and real estate) and across different industries or regions. The goal is to avoid putting all your money into one type of investment.
Why? Because if one investment loses value, others may perform well

and help balance out your losses. For example, if you have some money in tech stocks, some in bonds, and some in real estate, a downturn in tech stocks won't hurt your overall portfolio as much. Diversification helps smooth out the ups and downs of the market and makes your investments more stable.

4.2 How to Start with a Small Amount.

Getting into investing doesn't require thousands of dollars. You can absolutely start with a small amount and still make progress toward your financial goals. In fact, starting small gives you a chance to learn about investing without a big commitment, and over time, those small contributions can grow more than you might expect. Here's how to get started, even if you're only working with a little bit each month.

1. *Choose Low-Cost Investment Options.*
When you're starting with a smaller amount, high fees can quickly eat into your returns, so look for low-cost investment options. Exchange-traded funds (ETFs) and index funds are great choices because they're generally low-cost and offer instant diversification. These funds typically track a market index (like the S&P 500), which means your money is

spread across a broad range of stocks, reducing risk while keeping fees low.

Many brokers allow you to buy fractional shares of these funds, so even if an ETF share costs $100, you can buy a fraction for just $10 or $20.

2. Consider a Robo-Advisor
Robo-advisors are online platforms that help you build and manage an investment portfolio based on your financial goals, risk tolerance, and time horizon. They're affordable and easy to use, making them ideal for beginner investors who might feel overwhelmed by choosing investments themselves.

Here's how it works:
You sign up, answer a few questions about your goals, and the robo-advisor suggests a diversified portfolio for you.

They manage your investments for a small fee (often lower than traditional financial advisors).

You can start with as little as $100, or sometimes even less.
Robo-advisors automate the investing process and rebalance your portfolio as needed, so it's a "set it and forget it" option for those just getting started.

3. *Use Apps for Micro-Investing*

Micro-investing apps have made it incredibly easy to start investing with small amounts. These apps allow you to invest spare change or make small contributions on a regular basis. For example, some apps round up your purchases to the nearest dollar and invest the difference. If you spend $3.50 on coffee, the app rounds it up to $4 and invests the extra $0.50.

These micro-investing apps also let you set up recurring contributions as low as $5 or $10 a week, so you can build an investment habit without needing a large initial deposit. Over time, these small investments can add up.

4. Start with Retirement Accounts

If you're looking to invest with a long-term perspective, retirement accounts like a 401(k) (if your employer offers one) or an IRA are great places to start. Many 401(k) plans allow you to contribute a small percentage of your paycheck, which may be matched by your employer, doubling your investment automatically.

Employer Match: Some employers match your 401(k) contributions up to a certain percentage. So if you're only contributing a small amount, the match effectively doubles it.

IRA Contributions: You can start an IRA with a few hundred dollars and add small amounts whenever possible. The tax advantages make these accounts even more valuable in the long run.
Starting with retirement accounts allows you to invest in the stock market over a long period, letting compound interest work its magic.

5. *Make Small, Consistent Contributions*

Consistency is more important than the amount you start with. Small, regular contributions can grow significantly thanks to compound interest. If you can set aside even $25 a month, that's a great starting point.

The key is to stay consistent and, if possible, increase your contributions over time as your income grows. Set up automatic transfers to your investment account so that each month a small amount goes straight to your investments without needing to think about it. You'll be surprised how quickly it adds up.

CHAPTER FIVE

Building Income Streams

5.1 *Side Hustles and Passive Income Ideas.*

When it comes to achieving financial freedom, building multiple streams of income can be a game changer. Relying solely on a single paycheck often means you're limited in how much you can earn, and any unexpected job loss or pay cut could throw your finances off track. By diversifying your income sources, you add extra stability and boost your ability to save, invest, and grow wealth over time. Let's dive into a few popular side hustle ideas and passive income strategies that can help get you started on the path to financial independence.

1. Freelancing and Consulting
If you have skills in areas like writing, graphic design, programming, marketing, or finance, freelancing can be a powerful way to earn extra money. Many people start freelancing in their spare time and, over time, build it into a solid income stream. Platforms like Upwork,

Fiverr, and LinkedIn make it easier than ever to connect with clients.

Consulting is another option if you're an expert in a particular field, whether it's business, career advice, or fitness. By offering one-on-one consultations, you can leverage your experience to help others—and get paid well for it. The great thing about freelancing and consulting is that you have the flexibility to work on projects that fit your schedule.

2. Selling Products Online
E-commerce is booming, and selling products online has never been more accessible. Whether you want to create and sell handmade crafts on

Etsy, sell unused items on eBay, or dropship products through Amazon, there are countless ways to earn money online.

If you're creative, you could consider designing T-shirts, phone cases, or other merchandise through print-on-demand services like Redbubble or Teespring, which handle production and shipping for you. This allows you to earn income with minimal upfront costs, as you only pay for products once they're sold.

3. *Affiliate Marketing*
Affiliate marketing is a way to earn commissions by promoting products or services you believe in. When

someone purchases through your affiliate link, you get a small percentage of the sale. It's a common passive income strategy for bloggers, YouTubers, and social media influencers who want to monetize their audience.

To get started, you can join affiliate programs like Amazon Associates, ShareASale, or specific brands' programs. The key is to promote products that align with your content or interests, as this builds trust and increases the likelihood of earning commissions.

4. Rental Income

Owning rental property can generate steady passive income. If buying a property is feasible for you, renting it out can be a smart way to build wealth over time. With platforms like Airbnb, you could even consider renting out a room in your home to start generating income with minimal initial investment.

For those not ready to buy property, consider renting out other assets you already own, like your car on platforms like Turo or your camera gear, sports equipment, or tools through local rental marketplaces. It's a simple way to monetize things you aren't using all the time.

5. *Investing in Dividend Stocks.*

If you're interested in investing, dividend stocks can be a source of passive income. Certain companies pay dividends—small, regular payments to shareholders—typically on a quarterly basis. If you are investing in a portfolio of reliable dividend-paying stocks, you can earn income without having to sell your investments.

Dividends aren't guaranteed, and they can fluctuate based on company performance, but they're a popular choice for people who want their investments to generate regular cash flow.

6. *Digital Products*

Creating digital products like e-books, online courses, stock photos, or digital art can provide passive income with the potential for high returns. Once you've created a digital product, it can be sold repeatedly with minimal additional effort.

Platforms like Amazon Kindle Direct Publishing (for e-books), Udemy (for courses), and Shutterstock (for stock photos) make it easier to reach a large audience. If you're knowledgeable about a topic, consider turning it into a digital product that can continue to sell for months or even years.

7. YouTube and Blogging

If you enjoy creating content, starting a YouTube channel or blog can eventually become a profitable side hustle. While it might take time to build an audience, content creation can provide long-term passive income through ad revenue, sponsorships, and affiliate marketing.

YouTube monetizes through ads once you meet certain view and subscriber requirements, and a blog can earn money through Google AdSense, affiliate marketing, or sponsored posts. Both options require commitment, but they're great ways to turn a passion or interest into income.

5.2 Earning More in Your Free Time

Expanding your income streams doesn't always require a huge time commitment, nor does it mean adding loads of stress to your life. Like side hustles and passive income ideas, earning extra money in your free time can be done strategically and at a pace that fits your lifestyle. This approach allows you to experiment with income-generating activities during evenings, weekends, or any spare time without giving up your primary job or hobbies.

<u>Here are some effective ways to earn more on a flexible schedule:</u>

1. *Take Advantage of the Gig Economy*

The gig economy has made it possible to earn extra money whenever you're available, even if it's only for a few hours at a time. Companies like Uber, Lyft, and DoorDash let you drive or deliver food on your own schedule. If you're good with organization, you could even offer personal assistance or shopping services through platforms like TaskRabbit or Instacart.

Gig jobs allow you to work when you want and take breaks when you need them. You're not locked into a rigid schedule, and these jobs can be a quick way to bring in additional cash flow when needed.

2. *Remote Freelance Work*
While freelancing can be a major side hustle, you can also take on smaller, one-time projects that fit into your free time. Sites like Upwork, Fiverr, and even LinkedIn have sections for short-term or one-off jobs, which can be perfect if you're looking for something temporary. Many freelance gigs can be done in a few hours and allow you to leverage specific skills, like writing, graphic design, or social media management, to earn money without a long-term commitment.

If you're fluent in a second language, for example, you could offer quick translation services. Or, if you're tech-savvy, basic website troubleshooting or digital marketing advice could bring in extra income.

3. *Participate in Online Surveys and Market Research.*
Though online surveys won't make you rich, they're a straightforward way to earn a little extra during your free time. Sites like Survey Junkie, Swagbucks, and Pinecone Research pay you to answer surveys or participate in consumer research. It's something you can do while watching TV or during a break in your day.

Market research studies or focus groups generally pay higher rates than standard surveys. Some can be done remotely via phone or online chat, making them convenient, flexible options that only take an hour or two.

4. *Rent Out Your Space or Belongings*
If you have unused space in your home—a spare room, garage, or even a parking spot—you could rent it out for extra income. Platforms like Neighbor make it easy to rent storage space to locals who need it, and sites like Airbnb allow you to rent out an extra room to travelers. This can be an especially good option if you live in a high-demand area.

Or consider renting out belongings that you don't use all the time. If you own a bike, camera gear, or high-quality sports equipment, there are local rental services and apps where people can borrow them. This passive income can bring in cash without requiring much time or energy on your part.

5. *Monetize Your Hobbies*
If you have hobbies or skills you enjoy, consider finding ways to make money from them. Are you good at crafting, painting, or baking? Sites like Etsy allow you to set up a shop where you can sell handmade items. Or if you're into photography, you can sell stock photos online.

Monetizing a hobby can be one of the most rewarding ways to earn in your free time, as you're already doing something you love. Plus, if it becomes successful, you might even consider turning it into a larger side hustle.

6. *Virtual Tutoring or Teaching*
With the rise of online education, virtual tutoring has become a viable way to make extra money in a flexible manner. Platforms like VIPKid, Wyzant, or Tutor.com allow you to connect with students who need help in various subjects. You can choose when and how often you

want to teach, making it easy to fit sessions into your free time.

Whether you're skilled in a particular school subject, foreign language, or even music, tutoring is a great way to share knowledge while earning money. And, if you enjoy it, it can be a rewarding experience that adds to your professional skills.

7. *Pulling It All Together*
Just like side hustles and passive income ideas, earning more in your free time is about finding methods that complement your lifestyle, interests, and availability. From gig economy jobs and remote freelancing to monetizing hobbies and renting out

unused items, the options are as flexible as they are diverse. Think of this approach as a stepping stone toward your financial goals—a way to build your income stream by stream without overwhelming yourself.

CHAPTER SIX

Planning for the Future

6.1 Starting Your Retirement Fund Early

Let's talk about something most people in their 20s and 30s don't think about enough: retirement. I know it can feel so far away, and the thought of saving for it now may seem unnecessary, especially when there are so many immediate financial goals. But here's the truth: starting your retirement fund early is one of the smartest moves you can make for your future self.

When you start saving for retirement early, you're setting up a solid financial foundation that grows over time. You might not be able to stash away large amounts right away, but even small contributions can make a huge difference thanks to something called compound interest. This "magic" of compounding means that the money you invest today doesn't just sit there—it grows, and the growth itself starts to grow, creating a snowball effect.

Why Start Now?

Starting your retirement fund early isn't just about the amount of money you're putting aside; it's about giving that money as much time as possible to grow. Imagine putting in just a little bit each month in your 20s. Those contributions might not seem like much now, but fast forward 30 or 40 years, and they'll have multiplied several times over. On the other hand, if you wait until you're older to start saving, you'll need to contribute much more each month to catch up. Time is the most powerful asset when it comes to investing for the long term.

Where to Begin?

1. Understand Your Options – Start by learning about the types of retirement accounts available, whether they're employer-sponsored plans, personal IRAs, or even simpler options like regular investment accounts. Each comes with its own set of benefits, and choosing the right one will help you make the most of your contributions.

2. Employer-Sponsored Plans – If you're working for a company that offers a retirement plan like a 401(k), take advantage of it! Many companies offer matching contributions, which is essentially free money added to your retirement fund. Contribute at least

enough to get the full match, if you can.

3. IRAs – If you're not sure about employer plans or are self-employed, an Individual Retirement Account (IRA) can be a fantastic option. A Roth IRA, for instance, allows your contributions to grow tax-free, which means more money for you in the long run.

4. Automate Your Savings – One of the best strategies to build a retirement fund is to set up automatic contributions. This way, a portion of your income is invested directly into your retirement account every month

without you even having to think about it.

5. *Start Small, but Be Consistent* – You don't have to contribute large amounts. The key is consistency. Even if you can only afford $50 or $100 a month to start, that's okay! As you continue, you can increase your contributions as your income grows.

6.2 Financial Independence Basics

Now that we've talked about starting your retirement fund early, let's dive into the bigger picture: financial independence. Achieving financial independence isn't just about saving money; it's about creating a lifestyle where you're free to make choices based on what truly matters to you—not just your paycheck.

At its core, financial independence means having enough wealth and income streams to support your desired lifestyle without being dependent on a traditional job. This doesn't necessarily mean being a millionaire. For many, it simply means having enough financial security to live comfortably, cover life's unexpected expenses, and pursue passions or goals without the constant pressure to earn more.

So, where do you start? Here are some basics to keep in mind:

1. Set Clear Goals

Financial independence starts with knowing what you want out of life. Think about what financial independence would look like for you—whether it's the freedom to travel, pursue a dream career, spend more time with family, or retire early. With clear goals, you can break down the steps to get there and keep yourself motivated along the way.

2. Develop a Savings Habit

Saving money isn't just for retirement; it's a habit that supports your financial security today and in the future. Try to build an emergency fund that can cover three to six months' worth of living expenses. This fund will serve as your financial cushion and give you peace of mind, knowing you can handle unexpected costs without debt or stress.

3. Spend Mindfully

Reaching financial independence doesn't mean cutting out everything fun or living a frugal lifestyle you don't enjoy. It's about spending intentionally on things that add real value to your life and cutting back on the rest. Look for ways to save on everyday expenses without sacrificing your quality of life. Maybe it's cooking at home more often, cutting back on impulse buys, or finding free or low-cost hobbies.

4. Invest in Assets, Not Liabilities

To build wealth, focus on accumulating assets—things that grow in value or provide income over time. Examples of assets include stocks, real estate, or even a business. Avoid overloading on liabilities like excessive debt or luxury items that depreciate quickly. Learning to invest wisely in assets puts you on a faster track to financial independence.

5. Develop Multiple Income Streams

As we covered in the previous section on side hustles and passive income, having more than one source of income can accelerate your path to financial independence. From freelancing to investing, finding ways to bring in additional income—even if it's just a little extra each month—gives you more flexibility and resilience in reaching your financial goals.

6. Keep Learning

Financial independence is a long-term goal, and the financial world is always evolving. Staying educated on personal finance, investing, and economic trends helps you make smarter choices. You don't need to be a finance expert, but taking time to learn new strategies or adjust your plans as needed keeps you in control of your financial future.

BRINGING IT ALL TOGETHER

Financial independence is all about taking control of your financial life. It might sound complex, but the basics—saving, spending wisely, investing, and creating multiple income streams—are practical steps anyone can start taking. Each move you make, from setting goals to investing, brings you closer to the freedom to live on your own terms. And remember, every small step today builds the foundation for a future of financial independence.

CONCLUSION

As we wrap up this guide, let's take a moment to reflect on why you started this journey. Achieving financial independence, building wealth, and securing your future aren't things that happen overnight—they're the results of consistent effort, smart choices, and, above all, commitment. Every step you've taken so far, from budgeting and saving to investing and exploring new income streams, has brought you closer to a life where you're in control of your finances, rather than your finances controlling you.

The road to financial freedom isn't always easy, but it's incredibly rewarding. There will be ups and downs, temptations to splurge, or unexpected expenses. The key is to stay focused on your goals, adjusting as needed but never losing sight of the freedom you're building for yourself.

Final Tips for a Lifetime of Freedom

Here are some parting tips to keep you on track as you move forward:

1. Celebrate Small Wins – Financial freedom is a big goal, but don't forget to celebrate the small victories along the way. Paid off a credit card? Started investing? Build up your emergency fund? Take a moment to recognize your progress; it'll help you stay motivated.

2. Keep Learning and Adapting – Financial knowledge is power. The more you learn about managing money, the better equipped you'll be to make smart decisions. Stay curious, keep up with trends, and adapt your strategies as your life changes.

3. Review and Re-evaluate Regularly – Life changes, and so do financial goals. Take time every few months to assess your progress. Are you on track? Do you need to adjust your budget or increase your savings? Regular check-ins keep your goals fresh and attainable.

4. Stay Disciplined but Flexible – Discipline is key to reaching your financial goals, but so is flexibility. Life throws curveballs, and sometimes you'll need to adjust or take a different approach. Don't let temporary setbacks derail you;

instead, stay adaptable and keep moving forward.

5. Remember Your Why – When the journey feels tough, remember why you started. Visualize the freedom you're working toward, the security you're building, and the opportunities you'll create for yourself and your loved ones.

A Life of Financial Freedom Awaits

You've taken the first steps toward creating a life of financial independence, a life where you have the freedom to pursue your dreams without financial constraints.

Remember, every small effort adds up, and staying committed to this journey will lead to the financial peace and freedom you've envisioned. So, keep pushing forward, stay committed, and embrace each step as you create a future on your terms. Here's to a lifetime of freedom and financial success!

HAPPY READING!

www.ingramcontent.com/pod-product-compliance
Lightning Source LLC
Chambersburg PA
CBHW031428210526
45464CB00005B/2101